THE DECLARATION OF INDEPENDENCE

BY MARY MEINKING

Published by The Child's World®
1980 Lookout Drive • Mankato, MN 56003-1705
800-599-READ • www.childsworld.com

ACKNOWLEDGMENTS
The Child's World®: Mary Swensen, Publishing Director
Red Line Editorial: Editorial direction and production
The Design Lab: Design

Photographs ©: Victorian Traditions/Shutterstock Images, cover,
2; Red Line Editorial, 5, 17; Don Troiani/Corbis, 7; iStockphoto, 8,
12; GraphicaArtis/Corbis, 10; Joseph Sohm/Shutterstock Images,
15; George K. Warren/Corbis, 19; Matt York/AP Images, 20

ISBN 9781503809017
LCCN 2015958454

Printed in the United States of America
Mankato, MN
June, 2016
PA02309

On the cover: Benjamin Franklin, John Adams,
and Thomas Jefferson read the Declaration of
Independence.

TABLE OF CONTENTS

CHAPTER 1

THE AMERICAN COLONIES

Americans have many freedoms. Citizens can vote and hold political office. They can express opinions about government. Not all people have these freedoms. The founders of the United States fought for the rights we have today.

In the 1600s, Europeans settled in North America. Some wanted to farm, hunt, or trade. Others wanted to be free to practice their religion. In 1607, the British established a settlement in Virginia. It became their first North American **colony**. By the 1730s, Britain had 13 colonies in North America.

BRITISH SETTLEMENTS IN NORTH AMERICA

In 1607, Britain began a settlement in Jamestown, Virginia. Settlers raised crops. The people suffered at first. It took a long time to grow food on the new land. But eventually, the settlers succeeded. Britain established a colony in Virginia. By 1732, they had 13 colonies in North America.

YEARS THE COLONIES BEGAN

NEW HAMPSHIRE: 1638

NEW YORK: 1626

RHODE ISLAND: 1636

PENNSYLVANIA: 1682

MASSACHUSETTS: 1620

CONNECTICUT: 1636

NEW JERSEY: 1664

VIRGINIA: 1607

DELAWARE: 1638

MARYLAND: 1633

NORTH CAROLINA: 1653

SOUTH CAROLINA: 1663

Atlantic Ocean

GEORGIA: 1732

N

W   E

S

BOUNDARIES BY THE END
OF THE REVOLUTIONARY WAR (1783)

Gulf of Mexico

The British king, George III, ruled the colonies. Colonial governors carried out the king's laws.

At first, most colonists obeyed the king's laws. They did not mind being ruled by Britain. But the situation changed in 1754. In that year, a conflict began in the colonies. France and Britain fought over North American land. Native Americans also fought on both sides. The British helped protect the colonists' land. Until 1763, they fought the French and Indian War.

Britain won the war, but the conflict was costly. British leaders wanted the colonists to pay them for protecting the land. Colonists had to pay taxes on certain products. The products included tea, paper, and glass.

Colonists protested the new taxes. The colonists had no representatives in the British government. They had no say in the tax laws. Angry colonists chanted, "No taxation without representation." But Britain still collected taxes.

Soon, colonists decided to fight back. In December 1773, they took action. Hundreds of men from Massachusetts dressed as Native Americans. They sneaked onto British ships in Boston Harbor. These ships were carrying tea. The men dumped 342 crates of tea into the water. They were

**A teapot showed a message of protest against the
Stamp Act. This law taxed colonial products.**

protesting the tea tax. Today, we know this event as the
Boston Tea Party.

Britain punished Boston for the colonists' actions. The
government closed the city's port. A new law banned many
town meetings. A military government took control of
Massachusetts. These harsh laws angered the colonists.
Rebels refused to pay taxes. They would not buy British
products. Some hid weapons. If British forces attacked, they
wanted to defend themselves.

On April 19, 1775, British soldiers marched to
Lexington, Massachusetts. They planned to take away
rebels' weapons. But the colonists heard about this plan.

During the Boston Tea Party of 1773, colonists dumped crates of tea into Boston Harbor.

When the British arrived, Lexington rebels were ready. They stood with their weapons, waiting. Eventually, someone fired a shot. No one knew who fired it. But a battle quickly followed.

The Revolutionary War had begun. The 13 colonies united to form an army. They were fighting for freedom from Britain. Soon, colonists would announce their **independence**. And they would do so by publishing an official document.

CHAPTER 2

WRITING THE DECLARATION

By May 1775, the colonists were at war. But they needed to decide what to do next. There were 13 different colonies. To win the war, they needed to work together. Colonists could unite to form a new country.

Delegates from each colony began to meet. This group was known as the Second Continental Congress. They gathered in Philadelphia, Pennsylvania. Delegates planned the war effort. They united colonial militias into an army. They also talked about becoming independent from Britain. As a new country, they could decide their own laws.

Virginia delegate Richard Henry Lee proposed a **resolution**. The resolution said, "These United Colonies are . . . free and independent States." The group debated the issue. They would adopt the resolution only if all delegates agreed. Many delegates needed their home colonies to agree to the plan. They would take a vote in July 1776.

An 1817 painting by John Trumbull showed a
gathering of the Second Continental Congress.

Meanwhile, the congress began writing a **declaration**. If the resolution passed, the delegates would publish it. This document would announce the colonies' independence. Thomas Jefferson wrote the first **draft**. He was a member of the Continental Congress. Jefferson was also a lawyer.

On June 28, 1776, the group read Jefferson's draft. They carefully examined every word. Some parts were changed. The original draft mentioned slavery. But the founders of the nation disagreed on the issue. They did not know whether to allow slavery in the new country. The founders removed that part. Finally, they developed a version they all agreed on.

The Declaration of Independence had five parts. The first part was the introduction. The second part was the **preamble**. It said that people sometimes had to end political partnerships. When that happened, they needed to explain their reasons.

The third part described the colonists' ideas about government. It said that "all men are created equal." As a result, they had certain equal rights. These included the right to "Life, Liberty and the pursuit of Happiness."

The Declaration of Independence listed complaints against George III, the British king.

Governments needed to respect those rights. If they did not, the people could create a new government.

The fourth part listed 27 **grievances**. These were complaints against King George III. One was that the king had taxed the colonists. Another said that he had not allowed them to govern themselves. A third grievance was that he controlled the colonies' trade. They could not freely sell products to other countries. These were all reasons for separating from Britain.

The fifth part was the conclusion. It said that the colonies were an independent country. They would not follow British rule.

On July 2, 1776, it was time to conduct a vote. Delegates from 12 colonies voted to become independent. One colony, New York, did not vote. The New York delegates were waiting for news from colony officials. But their approval was on its way. Soon, the Declaration of Independence would take effect.

CELEBRATING INDEPENDENCE

July 4 is Independence Day. This holiday honors Americans' freedom. Delegates voted for independence on July 2, 1776. At first, Americans celebrated their independence on July 2. However, the Declaration is dated July 4, 1776. Eventually, the United States began celebrating on July 4 instead. This date became a national holiday in 1870.

CHAPTER 3

NEWS OF THE DECLARATION

Nearly all of the colonies had agreed to declare independence. However, few people knew about this decision. It was time to spread the news. Delegates would send the Declaration of Independence to officials. They would deliver it to newspapers. Some copies would go to reporters in Britain.

Printer John Dunlap made copies of the Declaration. These copies were known as the Dunlap broadsides. On July 5, they were sent throughout the colonies and abroad. But news traveled slowly. Messengers rode on horseback through the colonies. Copies traveled to other countries by ship. These journeys would take days or weeks.

On July 9, the Declaration reached New York City. Continental Army soldiers were staying nearby. George Washington was their commander. He read the text aloud at City Hall. Colonists gathered and cheered. The crowds ran to a local square. They tore down a statue of

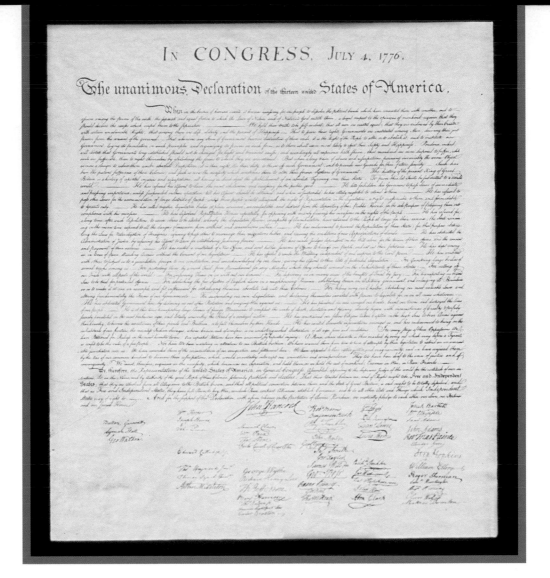

**In August 1776, delegates signed the official copy
of the Declaration of Independence.**

King George III. That same day, the New York delegates
finally heard from their home colony. They were allowed
to vote on the Declaration. The delegates voted for
independence. It was **unanimous**. All 13 colonies accepted
the Declaration of Independence.

Afterward, the 56 delegates signed a copy of the Declaration. This official copy was printed on **parchment**. John Hancock was the first to sign it. He signed his name in large, bold letters. Hancock hoped to give other delegates confidence. By signing the Declaration, they were committing treason. They were defying the king. Treason was punishable by death. But the delegates signed their names anyway.

Weeks later, the Declaration reached Britain. On August 10, 1776, the *London Gazette* reported on it. Other sources published the news soon afterward. King George III criticized the men who signed the Declaration. The king said they had given up "all **allegiance** to the crown, and all political connection with this country."

Still, the king wanted to keep colonial America. The British kept fighting. The war continued for seven years. General Washington's army was determined to win freedom. Finally, the British surrendered. The two sides signed the Treaty of Paris in September 1783. This treaty made it official. The United States was an independent nation.

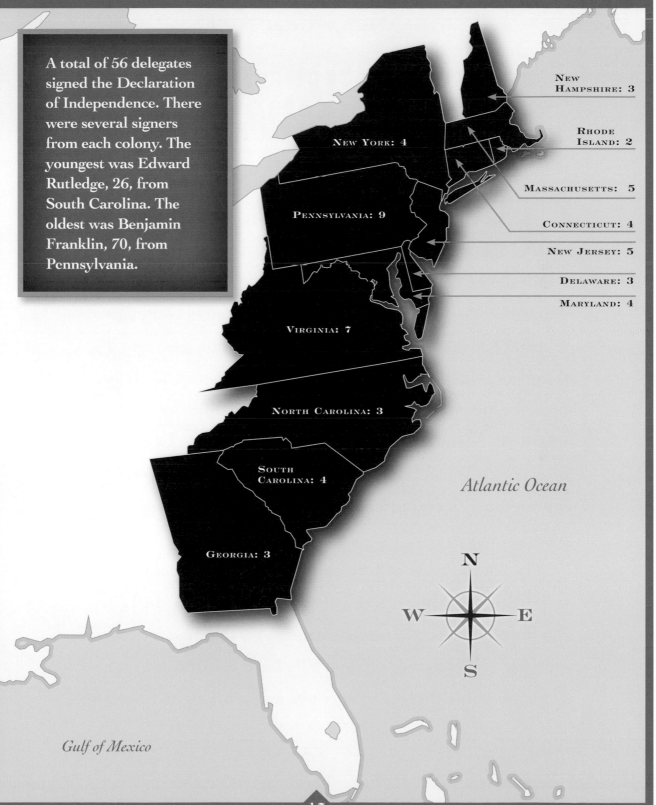

A total of 56 delegates signed the Declaration of Independence. There were several signers from each colony. The youngest was Edward Rutledge, 26, from South Carolina. The oldest was Benjamin Franklin, 70, from Pennsylvania.

NEW HAMPSHIRE: 3

RHODE ISLAND: 2

MASSACHUSETTS: 5

CONNECTICUT: 4

NEW JERSEY: 5

DELAWARE: 3

MARYLAND: 4

NEW YORK: 4

PENNSYLVANIA: 9

VIRGINIA: 7

NORTH CAROLINA: 3

SOUTH CAROLINA: 4

GEORGIA: 3

Atlantic Ocean

Gulf of Mexico

N

W   E

S

CHAPTER 4

FROM THE SIGNING TO TODAY

The United States was a new nation. It was the first to successfully declare independence from a founding country. But it would not be the last. The American Revolution inspired people in other countries.

In 1789, French rebels began a revolution against their king. In 1821, Mexico declared independence from Spain. One year later, Brazil declared independence from Portugal. Many in these countries admired the Declaration of Independence. Some also wrote declarations. Today, more than 120 countries have issued declarations of independence.

The Declaration of Independence did not create any laws. But it did help establish Americans' rights. In 1787, the founders wrote a **constitution**. This document described citizens' rights in more detail. The U.S. Constitution explained how the government would work. The first ten

Frederick Douglass worked to end slavery. He said that slaves should have the freedom the Declaration promised.

amendments, or changes, to the Constitution were the Bill of Rights. They spelled out Americans' freedoms.

Some Americans continued to fight for liberty. The Declaration said that "all men are created equal." However, slavery was allowed in the new country. Slaves were forced to work for no pay. They were separated from their families. Many faced harsh living conditions. Slaves wanted the liberty that the Declaration promised. Opponents of slavery worked to free the slaves.

Children view one of the earliest copies of the Declaration of Independence at a visiting museum exhibit in Phoenix, Arizona.

For decades, the United States faced conflicts over slavery. Some states outlawed it. Yet slavery continued in other states. In 1861, these conflicts led to the American Civil War. The war ended in 1865. Slavery was outlawed throughout the country. Former slaves had new rights. They could vote. They could earn money for their work.

Many women wanted equal rights, too. In the early United States, women were denied many freedoms. They could not vote or own property. In 1848, hundreds of women met in Seneca Falls, New York. They wrote the Declaration of Sentiments. This document was based on the Declaration of Independence. It promised rights for both women and men. The Declaration of Sentiments said that "all men and women are created equal."

Slowly, the laws changed. In 1920, American women reached a milestone. A new amendment passed. Women could vote throughout the United States. They had new rights and liberties.

WHERE IS THE DECLARATION OF INDEPENDENCE?

The signed Declaration traveled across the nation. It was displayed in Pennsylvania, Maryland, New Jersey, and New York. In 1800, the Declaration moved to Washington, DC. It is still there today. The document moved only during World War II. In wartime, officials wanted to keep the document safe. They hid it in Fort Knox, Kentucky.

Today, the Declaration still inspires Americans. People celebrate this document every Fourth of July. Presidents use its words in their speeches. Most of all, people honor the ideas of liberty and equality from the Declaration of Independence. These ideas helped make the United States a free, independent nation.

allegiance (uh-LEE-juns) Allegiance is loyalty to a country or leader. King George III wanted the allegiance of the colonists.

colony (KOL-uh-nee) A colony is a territory owned by another nation. Virginia was the first British colony in North America.

constitution (kon-sti-TOO-shun) A constitution explains the basic laws of a nation. The constitution of the United States was based on the Declaration of Independence.

declaration (dek-luh-RAY-shun) A declaration is a document that makes a public announcement. The Declaration of Independence announced that the 13 colonies were a united, free nation.

delegates (DEL-i-gits) Delegates are people who represent a place or group. In the Continental Congress, delegates represented each of the 13 colonies.

draft (DRAFT) A draft is a version of a document. Thomas Jefferson wrote the first draft of the Declaration of Independence.

grievances (GREE-vun-ses) Grievances are complaints, or reasons for being upset. The Declaration of Independence listed 27 grievances about King George III.

independence (in-di-PEN-duns) When people have independence, they are free from outside control. The 13 American colonies wanted independence from Britain.

parchment (PARCH-munt) A parchment is a special material made from animal skin. The official, signed copy of the Declaration of Independence is written on parchment.

preamble (PREE-am-bul) A preamble is a beginning part of a document or text. The Declaration of Independence includes a preamble.

rebels (REB-ulz) Rebels are people who fight against their own country or leader. Many American colonists became rebels against the British king.

resolution (rez-uh-LOO-shun) A resolution is the formal statement of a group's decision. Richard Henry Lee wrote a resolution that the 13 colonies should break away from Britain.

unanimous (yoo-NAN-uh-mus) If something is unanimous, all of the people in a group agree on it. The vote to seek independence from Britain was unanimous.

TO LEARN MORE

IN THE LIBRARY

Landau, Elaine. *The Declaration of Independence*. New York: Scholastic, 2008.

Sirimarco, Elizabeth. *Thomas Jefferson*. Mankato, MN: The Child's World, 2009.

St. George, Judith. *The Journey of the One and Only Declaration of Independence*. New York: Philomel, 2014.

ON THE WEB

Visit our Web site for links about the Declaration of Independence: **childsworld.com/links**

Note to Parents, Teachers, and Librarians: We routinely verify our Web links to make sure they are safe and active sites. So encourage your readers to check them out!

INDEX

ABOUT THE AUTHOR

Mary Meinking has written more than 30 children's books. The topics of her books include history, arts and crafts, extreme jobs, animals, pop stars, and travel. When not working or writing, Meinking enjoys spending time with family, making crafts, baking, and traveling. She lives in Iowa.